BREAK FREE

A POETRY COMPILATION OF
A BROKEN HERITAGE
RESTORED

LEROY PEOPLES JR.

By david-cantelli @unsplash

RELATIONSHIPS

Case Number 1-7154181631 November 20, 2018
Registered with the United States of America Copyright Office

TABLE OF CONTENTS

MAMA

God is Love and God made mother

You treated us special

not like any other

You taught us to pray

before we went to sleep

Cause a young hard head

could make you weep

You kept us fed, you kept us warm

Your arms protected us

from the storms

When we became older

we knew what to do

and passed on to our sons, daughters, and grandchildren

what we learned from you

To love and cherish

our families today

with exemplary values

cause you loved us that way

THE BIRTH OF LAKESHA MARIE

Lakesha was born premature

a one pound nine ounces miniature

She is a tiny child of the light

a fragile flower growing through the storm

A little one born in pain

that's part of my family

She is a little honey saved from the hive

a mysterious miracle before my eyes

that's my responsibility

I pray your days and nights find peace

Sheltered from this barren world

Why do I care so much for you?

Cause, you are more precious than any pearl

LOVE

Heaven planted the seed

of our unconditional love

Love grows like a palm tree

Two souls yearning to start a family

We have our own garden

May our love bloom?

And blossom efflorescence

in our own room

Yes, hard times came

as the family grew

One child almost died

but love stayed true

Keep the family growing?

Don't let the tree die

While passing through our storms

to divorce we said bye-bye

HONEY

Honey, can I read your thoughts?

Open your heart to me

Let me hear the music

in your mind's melody

Honey, I'm sorry I rejected you

I'm just a complicated man
You are so sweet and tender
let me hold your hand

Somehow, we got lost
in the matrices of this life
Pressures and problems
only brought in more strife

Honey, I can't read your mind
Take all the love you need from me
Let me break the code
and love you from A to Z

Upload all your fantasies
Way deep down into my heart
Don't you see what we're missing?
Let's begin a new start

For Her

A bouquet of flowers

picked among the dandelions

in an open field

kissing a clear sky

A butterfly dance near

the myrtle trees

as I hear the music

from the busy bumblebees

Visiting each flower as if

each one's the last

inhaling their nectar

before the sunlight's passed

I survey calmly

the scenery

of a blue jay perched

in an old maple tree

While the blowing wind

plays a melody

in the open field's

musical symphony

A bouquet of flowers

picked among the dandelions

for my dear wife

a precious love of mine

A GOOD FEELING

A peaceful day

with a sunny heart

A moonlit evening

A stroll in the park

Two hearts beating

with one sound

Love surrounds us

like there's no one around

Breathing the fresh spring air

Holding hands

with the one who cares

Eye to eye

Face to face

With the special one

who knows her place

in my life

until our last sunset

in my life

Because she's my wife

in God we met

MAN AND WOMAN

Passionate love in the shadows
Whispering secrets with a kiss
Unknown pleasure made known
Fulfilled in fantasies of liquid bliss

Bathing in this wine-filled moment
as honey drips from her breasts
Puddles of warm milk sweating
cinnamon juices in her nest

Bliss speaks through moments of joy
Vibrating rhythms in pelvic places
Kissing the softness of her tongue
Removing her dew moist laces

The body yearning for an encore
In her rose-filled bed
May this moment never end
as you move your tongue across my head

Ebony beauty within my arms

Smelling her perfumed hair

Her tiny waist beckons me

like the taste of a juicy pear

Your inhibitions thrown to the wind

allowing me to have complete control

With every sound of approval

blending our hearts with our souls

ROMANCE AND MUSIC

See me through the window of your heart

in the fragrant flower of your love

Play a melody so bright

on wings like a soaring dove

You are glowing in my thoughts

with an ecstasy unknown

Count the petals of a rose

and have them gently blown

In the place that's made for me
gentle mountains where love grows
Taste the honey from the heart
in a way which no one knows

No one else will understand
Heart to heart and soul to soul
A magnetic warm embrace
pulsating sparks of costly gold

From the waters of the stream
flows an ecstasy unknown
A growing diamond full of light
and a lovely picture never shown

Let me whisper in your ear
words of passion divine
and kiss the dew from your lips
smelling of warm sweet wine

THINK

Laugh hearty, play in the sun

Swim in the crystal blue waters

Scuba dive in the coral reefs

Enjoy the time like you oughta

Feast your eyes on the majestic

island paradise

Soak in the sun

Don't forget your drink with ice

But the next day

something seems changed

It's hard to explain

The blue sky seems rearranged

What caused this change?

I know not why

Perhaps it's something

falling from the sky

PIECES OF TRUTH

Pieces of truth

gallop like a horse

Captured by the strong

used without remorse

Pieces of truth

rocking in a chair

on a moonlit night

clear and fair

Pieces of truth

reinvented for a cause

Sign the dotted line

but beware the hidden clause

Pieces of truth

from the beginning 'til now

changes and rearranges

like the devil with a vow

Pieces of truth

become a strong snare

like an endless puzzle

a game we must bear

Pieces of truth

that you remind me soar

Not enough pieces

to walk out the door

Pieces, pieces, everywhere

hidden unknown lights

covering the truth within

hidden out of sight

Let's all come together

with our pieces tonight

and place them together

'til it shines a new light

By shalom-mwenesi @unsplash

ENLIGHTENMENT

BEFORE ENLIGHTENMENT

As I stand alone in my solitude

I wonder why I exist

Just to take the pains of human suffering

and all troubles amidst?

It is nice for one to die his death

and let the wounds of anguish suffice

But hell, for one to die inside

and remains his life

To once enjoy charming delights

and companions of many

Desperately I ponder oh dear friend

but there isn't any

Self-pity overcame the reign of my pride

and I began to crumble like a century old monument

Left without hope, denied peace of mind

I longed for an escape to calm my lament

21

RESCUED

I trusted you, I was in your care

Free from pain and worry

I needed to be trained

I needed to be sheltered from the rain

There was only you

Where I should go

I believed that you loved me so

How could I know?

Something was wrong

Until I heard you play that song

I was made a victim all along

Look what you've done

You've brought the rain

My innocence is violated

Why draw me into your pain?

What will you gain?

Did you count the cost?

I'll rise above you I won't be lost

Even if I tell you will just deny

Convincing others I told a lie

But you will never understand why

I left when I could and never said goodbye

MY HEAVENLY FATHER

More real than the air I breathe

More present than the things I see

More mysterious than the north wind

He is the reason I exist

Everything must pay tribute to Him

All things are subject to Him

They grow old, but He remains forever

All His enemies perish daily

He has no beginning and no end

All things are created by Him alone

He answers only to Himself

Because He is the Highest Almighty

All men should fear, obey, and honor Him

And praise Him alone – worship only Him

Magnify His marvelous Name

esteem Him above all things

Obey His laws and commandments

and all His precepts and judgements

His beloved people are the Israelites

Hidden in scripture, read Leviticus 26 and Deuteronomy
28 tonight

Only one people on Earth and in the scriptures match

the curses in the book and sufferings to this day

And they are not European or Arabs, or other nations

They are the so-called Negro/African Americans

The secret of secrets, hidden in plain sight

Belong to the Highest Almighty's possession and
inheritance

They are the apple of His eye, and His precious jewels

Your future is based on how you treat Him and them

JANE DOE #1

I have a lover who is loving to me, but he is not my
husband

My husband controls too much, I feel like I'm in an oven

The fire doesn't burn anymore for him, I wonder if it ever
did

I married because I was getting old

And for my kid to learn a man's role

What shall I do now?

I'm in a mid-life crisis

I got to do something before the creek rises

Oh, I think what could have been if I had the chance

to have the one I truly love – a red velvet romance

With a man that's not weird or a little crazy too

That doesn't do strange things like an animal in a zoo

For now, I must exhale and hide my secret life

Cause my husband is crazy walking around with a knife

I guess my story must end, unfulfilled and gory

So, if you see me smile

Know that's not the true story

COLOR

What color is loyalty?

What color is hope?

Can we forget mercy?

Justice and truth.

What color are principles, valor, and prayer?

What color is the wind?

What color is the rain?

What color is insanity?

What color is pain?

What color is happiness?

What color are feelings?

Or the color of the human soul?

Or the color of healing?

Soon when the Almighty rules and reigns

the only color of men

then will be

a color of righteousness

WHITE PLACES THROUGH BLACK FACES

White places through black faces

Black faces with white minds

Teaching our lost children

The soul of another kind

Building the fence stronger

Enemies from within

Lost connection with our fathers

working against your kin

Eating Roman-ish Greek philosophies

You're disconnected soul parroting

What Massa approves, you say

While the children are perishing

Reconnect your poor soul

Find the courage to press on

Hear the ancients of old

The patriarchs in the ancient scrolls

The Messiah Black, Bold, Mighty, and Strong

Will want us all to give an accounting

and not to stumble His little ones

For silver and gold amounting

To white places through black faces

Black faces with white minds

Teaching our lost children

The soul of another kind

By andre-adjahoe @ unsplash

INDIGENOUS ABORIGINAL LANDS

Telling the truth and making someone cry, is better than telling a lie to make someone smile – Paulo Coelho

Shinnecock Tribe New York Times Image Archives 1895

Indigenous Aboriginal Copper-Colored People of Americas

African Americans are the Indigenous Copper-Colored People and the True blood-line Children of Israel

THEFT OF A LAND

Theft of a land

I did nothing wrong

I killed and enslaved

the copper-colored people

Except the ones who worship me

I changed their nationality

I added my DNA and paleness to some of their stock

by rape, sodomy, and Christianity

They must wait and wait and wait

to go to heaven

but I take everything

by my power right now

I protect my wickedness

with my unlawful laws

and my unlawful courts

I massacred them on their own land

I conquered them and brainwashed their minds

I changed their culture and stole their history

I redlined them and racially profiled them

and refused to give them an honest loan

In their own land

they are a proverb and a byword

I stole their legacy and their soul

and their end is planned

The source of everything positive I have come from them

I didn't know how to survive on this land

They helped me, taught me, and fed me

They willingly shared what they have

An honorable, wise, spiritual, and kind people

They will make good slaves for me

I'll change the truth of history

and blame Africa and the Africans for this

The truth of the whole matter

is they being already here in their own land

They are the true aboriginal, indigenous people

I stole it, I took this land, now it is mine

The history, I wrote and printed is full of lies
I replaced their superior culture with my face
Because I decide who lives and who dies
Now smile and sing my national anthem to my flag

Yes, I stole your land
But I don't feel I did anything wrong
Yes, I killed, raped, and enslaved your people
They were only copper-colored people

I stripped them bare of their royal status
and I forbade them to speak their ancient tongue
But they would not serve me from their hearts
so, I gave them Christianity and a White god to worship

Now I will remain supreme in their minds forever
because the god I taught them to worship looks like me
If some of them should discover that I stole their books
written by their own ancestors, who will believe them?

These are my niggers, and they shall remain my niggers
Just look at them, listen to them, they are lost

They are clueless to the fact that they are supposed to rule

and they listen to false prophets, politicians, Hollywood,
and demonic music

Most of them say they are Christians, which is our
invention

but they refuse to believe Leviticus 26 and Deuteronomy
28

If they found out the hidden secret to reverse the curse

And that their path to freedom is written in the ancient
scriptures

Checkmate

IGNORANCE WON'T CHANGE THE TRUTH

Lounging while watching the television

Lethargically putting off making decisions

Stupefied from the vibrations piercing my mind

Sensation-stimulated signals to hypnotize me

Through new images invading my thoughts

clouding my belief system and critical thinking

By a source not interested in the truth

working to control my mind

Not only my mind but also my dollars

Is there a systematic indoctrination process

to dumb down my critical thinking

and replace it with sports, news, and movies?

I am called a Negro, Black man, colored, African American

Should it not be more important to me

to finally find out who the hell I am?

What is the big mysterious secret?

I am too busy to research about

the actual truth about me

If I truly did what would I find out?

Would it not be a good thing if I found out the truth?

REPOSSESSING MY HAPPINESS

I'm repossessing my happiness
stolen for many years
I'm making amends to forgive
and to dry up my tears

I'm repossessing my happiness
sticking with my friend
Who has been with me from the beginning
and will stay to the end

I'm repossessing my happiness
I'm looking straight ahead
No time to entertain
how I'm being led

I'm repossessing my happiness
My heart is free
My soul is joined
to the Almighty and me
I'm repossessing my happiness
Don't worry about me

We've had many opportunities

now just let me be

VICTORY OVER THE THIEF

When a thief steals a car and does not have the keys.

He breaks into the vehicle and usually hot wires the ignition.

Thousands of years ago, it is written, that a thief stole control of the earth.

The earth was given to earthmen, who had a contract with the Almighty Creator.

This thief outsmarted almost all the earthmen and began to rule over the earth.

This thief wanted his DNA to spread among the earth people so he and his posse

began to spread their evil DNA by impregnating the earth's females.

They produced a new species with their own DNA.

This thief and his posse lost their position and status with the Almighty Creator.

They could no longer leave the flat earth dome, so the thief's anger and jealousy of the Creator's image drove him to seek an insane form of revenge against the sons of Adam while recruiting some of the people who live on the earth to assist him.

Now, the Almighty Creator is ending the thief's existence on the earth and is removing everything that offends Him and His kingdom rule on the earth. The thief and his posse are terrorized with the thought of their ultimate demise. One main principle they do understand is that the Almighty Creator does not lie.

THE VISIBLE MADE INVISIBLE

The visible made invisible

Dressed in naked scorn

With eyes burning from lack of rest

Searching for an unknown village

With a rainbow in the sky

Hiding from a new thunderstorm

Over a nameless ghetto

Made legal by a kangaroo court

That's hidden but working in harmony

To keep the visible invisible

Keeping them lost in an unjust maze

In a waterless mirage in the sand

REMEMBER MY CLEVELAND

Remember my Cleveland

79th and Kinsman, 1964

Garden Valley, Port Street playground and more

St. Theresa Holiness and Red's pool bar

Lawson's milk and bread and Vietnam War

Councilman's John never lost a race

Even with signs of deterioration all over the place

Families being daily divided

The recession has decided

The family nucleus is broken

Destiny has spoken

The head is severed

The remains are weathered

Trying to find the sun

With no place to run

Thanks to a new redlined community

The suburbs advance with impunity

With a full court press against us, do we really stand a
chance?

Some read the good book but has religion helped?

Even those who preach peace, heads are being scalped

I must confess, someone has done a good job

Our precious community is barren and robbed

Some bleeding hearts with consciousness came to the fore

While other communities are building castles, but ours – a dusty floor

If there is right in this universe, soon we will see

The Almighty's verdict on man, His tenant, children's prayers to be free!

I NEED TO HEAR FROM HEAVEN

I need to hear from heaven

cause I'm tired of listening to you

Filling our airwaves

with your version of truth

Like you can change water into wine

Masquerading as one divine

with many simple ones on your side

Cause you mixed their water with fluoride

How creative you are

A star without any twinkle

A little truth with a huge wrinkle

So, stop killing my sons

Darth Vader with a gun

Hidden behind a smiling face

Leprous Tools with a human taste

To stop you, we just need to know

Who has all the money?

Yes, follow the money

Follow the money

Follow the money

Follow the money

Follow the money

Fractional lending

Freedom is ending

Sixty-six aces in your deck

In debt with you up to our necks

TRUTH

I see the truth in your lies

The truth that is left out

of your truth will surely set me free

Truth, be not an enemy or stranger

but unveiled through being

matched with the desire to know

Being above the compromised

from the beginning, even century by century

Was it held tight by a few?

But is it allegories and signs?

Is there a way to secure the truth?

And, when will it just be made plain?

Not like a needle in the haystack anymore?

When will the curtain fall on so much drama?

WHITE FOR BLUE

Murder in the streets again
Was it someone in blue?
All the blame is on the dead man
The scene arranged to make that true

Did the dead man lying on the ground
attack or threaten anyone?
Or was he just running away from you,
scared as hell of your gun?

His running away triggered an instinct
living deep within your soul
Shoot first and cover up later
We hate these people from days of old

We've killed them in the north and south
We were slave catchers in those days
We have changed white for blue
Culling niggers is good pay

Today, we've hit the jackpot

We are harvesting organs from each one

We also make record profits

and in the process, we have some fun

THE PLAN FOR NEGROES

Unfruitful dreams in the darkness of night
wrest away my peaceful sleep
Once again, I'm placed in a nightmare
watching characters' fleece like innocent sheep

Why do I see such agonizing pictures
that are so livid and surreal?
People are forced to engage in unbelievable things
I can't imagine how they feel

Who is the director of my dreams?
Are they from heaven or from hell?
Or is it a sign of what's to come?
I sigh, but I cannot tell

I see the unthinkable arriving
Trying to swallow an unprepared soul
Our chickens have come to roost
and the plans will now unfold

Come out of her, my people

America has a place for you in this land

Many of you Negroes have never heard

of the King Alfred Plan

THE CARAT

They say, we are dangling this carat for you

See how attractive and dazzling it looks

Come, my good fellow and possess it

As soon as I reach out to grasp it

Mysteriously, it moves away

Like moving a goal post

Like changing the rules

In the middle of a game

Few can hold the carat

And those who do are warned

That you may hold it but never own it

You are not part of the committee

If you desperately want to hold it

And be counted as one of the few

You must pay a price

And follow their sordid rules

Come before three doors and choose

A blood sacrifice of one you love

Accept demonic penetration of your private flesh

Or say the hell with them and seek the HIGHEST
ALMIGHTY

DECEIVERS

The deceived deceivers

marching to their doom

Like actors in a masterpiece

a bride without a groom

Every joker playing its part

in this new world drama

The invisible referees take notes

to ensure your date with karma

It's hard to cover your mountain of lies

sowed for hundreds and hundreds of years

Increasing the use of mind control

Spreading lies as truth, with death, and fear

Your time is limited and short

The Highest Almighty One will not allow

you to continue corrupting His creation

The Almighty bidding you shall bow

You deceivers are deceived

marching to your doom

Like actors in a masterpiece

charging to your tomb

All the schemes you originate

fueled by your insane love for money and wealth

You sick, soulless, demonic beasts

Nothing will save yourself

By Jordan-woznia @unsplash

FAITH

THE WHIP AND THE BIBLE

The whip and the bible

helps Massa to teach me

to forget my culture and identity

and make him god, you see

Inventing/picking up behind him

making sure he won't fail

I be good to my Massa

or he will whip my tail

I don't have a tail

Wonder why he said that before

I ain't no monkey

I keep two feet on the floor

Lula Belle, my wife

is working in the kitchen

Cooks and cleans Massa's house

I thought I should mention

The last baby she had

don't look like me

If I complain about it
you'll see me hanging from a tree

I want to be a good boy
and make Massa glad
The bible says I'll go to heaven
He is the best Massa I ever had

Before you laugh at this man
and think you are tough stuff
Remember in the last century
we sat in the back of the bus

Do you know how you got here?
There is no need to fear
You were taken from Americas
because we were already here

The whip and the bible
has done its job well
To all who oppress us we say
Go to HELL

PASTOR

Pastor, pastor, pastor

Are you a title or a function?

Have you taught the people

who they were before so-called slavery?

You should boldly proclaim

who our ancestors are

Before four hundred years of so-called slavery

If you are chosen and blessed to know

If you cannot or will not articulate that truth

fold up your tent and go

and learn that truth

Stop buck dancing for the Massa

Don't be an imposter

See how it feels to be a real man

If you are called and chosen

Tell the whole truth

The Bible is not everybody's history

The Bible is the so-called negro history
We are the Almighty's chosen people
before Christianity was invented

Don't let any of your people
die without knowing the whole truth
Stop preaching and teaching lies
Repent pastor, and be set free

I dare you to research the lies you teach
Swallow your pride and teach people
To come out of Babylon, the whore
and you take the lead, bringing them out

TO WHOM IT MAY CONCERN

Who can stop Him?

Is it your missiles pointed toward the sky?

Are you safe in your underground homes

and your network of underground cities?

All beings are subject to His sovereign power

Both the living and the dead

will be judged by His laws, commandments, statues, and judgements

The time you have is like a rope

The rope is long but has an end

with an unbreakable noose

It has eternal consequences

and unlimited eternal Almighty power

In the days of old

He destroyed a complete powerful army

He also destroyed one hundred eighty-five thousand soldiers, who woke up dead

How can you use your weapons while you die?

All super computers obey His command

His chariots will appear through the skies

while all His precious jewels are removed and are safe

Now you are on your own

He who sits in the heavens shall laugh

He shall have you in derision

He shall speak to you in His wrath

and vex you in His displeasure

and exalt His sons over you

All your insurance policies

are worthless, null, and void

You are a confederacy of the damned

Creatures of destruction marked for eternal death

You who changed His laws

You who changed His Name

You who whited-out His people's history

You who assumed ownership of the earth you didn't create

You who bear false witness

You who dishonor His Name, and His chosen people

You who worship idols and doctrines of men

You who pollute His Sabbath

You who make graven images

You who dishonor your parents and your bodies

You who covet His creation and possessions

You who murder His people

You who enslaved His people

You who stole His people's land

You who stole His people's wealth

You who pollute the graves

of our fathers and elders

You who rob their grave sites

to enhance your false supremacy

You cannot stop Him

Your weapons are dust to Him

He who is in the heavens laughs at you

You are fools with pride

You all are soulless beasts

having intercourse with bloodthirsty reptiles

The Almighty will recompense you

To eternal fire and brimstone forever

TITHERS

Serving people in view of the cameras

Acting in front of the lens

Preaching with religious fervor

I got to make payments on my new Benz

Come on up to the altar

Choir don't sing that long

I need some more tithers

I'll lead the last song

After the service

I greet as many as I can

But I'm getting a little tired

while shaking all these hands

My, there's Sister Jenkins

fitting well in that tight dress

I'm trying not to look too hard at her

Man, she got some large xxxx

Poor little Sister Dupree

Her offering is too poor
But we need more faithful tithers
Coming through our doors

I guess I'll take my ministry
on national TV
to reach more tithers
That will get more money for me

We need a new building
The one we have is too small
And a brand-new location
With new seating and all

I also need a studio
to prepare my DVD's
A larger office
and a younger secretary

I still need to expand
I need a jet
to open new areas
We are no longer in debt

The bank accounts are filling up

We have increased our net

And with all these pagan holidays

a brand-new house I will get

I'm so busy with all this work

I have much to do

But for these non-tithers

I got no time for you

RELIGIOUS PUPPET

Don't be a pastor's puppet
Research all things
Don't make him a king
See what your labor will bring

Contact the Most High
through fervent prayer
Make the Almighty your King
Your burdens He will bear

Put all men in their place
under the Most High
No way can a man help you
when it's your time to die

The simple ones follow the crowd
listening to their tales
But for me and my house
our souls are not for sale

CHANGES

Weep before you cry and wail before you moan

The destruction of Babylon is at hand

Their sins have reached up to heaven

and are the center of the problems in my life

Many changes in my life; many, many, changes in my life

My heart became cold as ice and I thought I was to blame

I hated myself and felt powerless to change

From all the damage and scars I had as a child, teenager,
and Vietnam veteran

Divorced from a terribly bad marriage, bankruptcy, racism

No true knowledge of self-worth and beaten daily

With negativity, despair, hate, and lack of respect and love

Pain, misery, and suffering, because I'm poor and black

Hated by the whites and hated by the blacks

I'm just a lost child of Babylon, I'm finished before I
begun

Some have said that all roads lead to Rome

All my roads lead to darkness and death

Because even my relatives hate me without a cause

I hate you, because I can hate you

and there is nothing you can do to change it

Zero friends, plus many haters, equals hell

How in the hell do I get out of this hell in Babylon?

I lived in this pit of hell through many changes

But, now the gates of heaven are opened to me

This is the new change in my life!

A PROPHET'S PRAYER

Remove the destroyers of the earth

Cause enmity between them

I heard a rumor from within

that all destroyers will be destroyed

A fire is kindling in a secret place

being made ready to burn

All their wicket plans will not change

Their coming destruction which shall be swift

So, the earth can smile again

With one language and one king

The Creator Power Almighty Most High

knows what is best for all He has made

His true chosen ones and faithful servants

will receive their rewards

Rejoice and see the complete slaughter

of the destroyers of the earth

Those who hate His laws and commandments

will have no place to go or live

and all the religious institutions

will be removed from the earth

LEAVEN

Who is like the Almighty

but not the Almighty? Who is it?

It keeps the congregation to itself

Away from the one accord

There is a structure tried and strong

Lasting through many generations

When there is a decision to be made

it receives the topmost consideration

We've done things this way for years!

With plans for many more

Who are you, anyway

to expose what's in our store?

We have multiplied all over this land

Come unto us and lend a hand

You'll find a comfortable place to sit down

We'll work to keep your presence around

Give us your families and your friends

We'll teach them right to the very end

Put your name on our roll

We want to help save your soul

In the Book of Revelation

The Almighty hates the works of the Nicolaitans

and the teachings of Balaam and Jezebel

He that has an ear, let him hear well...

WORDS

Give us smooth words

not true

We want words to make us happy

Sweet words we've never heard

We will deal with truth later

like we never do

We will forget about it

Our stubbornness sticks like glue

I love my itching ears

My mind is on my dreams

I am always busy

but something in my heart screams

Urging me to consider why

the world is not my friend

I have experienced many broken promises

that have left me with emptiness and sin

I don't know why I hate the truth

What can I do to change me?

Is it written in the Scripture?

The truth shall make you free

We need true words

not smooth words

Such as Christianity, which is a lie

The greatest lie that's ever been told

We have been bewitched

Forced to receive this lie to behave

Which is a complete European invention

from their culture, to control their slaves

Come out their Babylonian teaching, that hates

to obey the Almighty's commandments and laws

Read, study, and meditate, and you will see

many other verses reveal their flaws

DISILLUSIONED CHURCH FOLKS

Do we have only one life?

If so, do we live a life

or do we live the truth?

Do we know the difference?

One thing we do know

We are alive and walking on the earth

Some say, I want to go to heaven

and at the same time, I don't want to die

Why would heaven want you?

Do you believe and seek to live?

The Almighty's laws and commandments

Do you accept the Almighty's Kingdom requirements?

A John 3:16 ticket will not get you anywhere

because the whole New Testament is a fable

Written by the Kalpournios Piso family

Seriously, research the true authors of the New Testament

When you find the Abelard Reuchlin history book

on the true authorship of the testament

Be in or close to a chair, so you won't fall

Tell your brothers and sisters, we have much work to do

LIES

My mind is filled with images
Most of these images are based on lies
Where is pure and eternal truth?
Why does truth show its face and then hide?

My mind is filled with dreams
Most of my dreams are lies
Why do I dream so much?
It is because reality makes me cry?

Each day, my mind, images, and dreams
continue to deceive and tell me lies
Some books, media, religion, people, and rulers
create their truth from fables, before my eyes

My reality changes from a lie, to another lie
My life is filled with many lows and highs
My road and path have been a circle that comprises
Going and coming and returning to my circle of lies

No matter where I have lived

I have only one address

Zero, zero, zero, lie street

Now, I'd like to have some rest

DEBT

Invisible tears roll down from my eyes

My heart pounds, and aches

from the thoughts and images in my mind

I feel like I am treading water

and my hopes and dreams

of being delivered from debt

is slowly fading away

No matter how hard I pray and work

debt seems to be glued to my soul

I am stuck within a dark cloud

and living in a fishbowl of despair

I am doomed if I do this plan

and doomed if I don't try to escape

the walls of this prison of debt

Oh learn, young people

from my foolish choices and mistakes

Learn to be fearless in protecting

and keeping what is yours

Learn all the pitfalls and loopholes

in this earth's legal and banking system

Before it is too late

CHANGE MY NAME

Reading poetry sitting in my favorite chair
The smell of silence is like fresh air
My mind is in a good place
My coffee is smooth to the taste

This evening seems especially calm
I must remember to set the alarm
What if things could stay like this
and I'd not have to deal with her honey-do list?

The poetry stimulated my thinking
What in the world were people drinking?
I wonder who can be blamed
To have the nerve to change my name

There are sick people, we all know
Some morals are quite barbaric and low
We are all tested in this human race
But to change another's name, what a disgrace

Maybe I should think of something good?

But how can it be understood?

To change someone else's name

without permission, are you insane?

It's too late to hide this sin

I guess your situation must have been

insecure paranoid and afraid

To leave your home and lead a raid

On another man's land

Sending a ruthless band

Those who are paranoid and schizophrenic

You need therapy from the heavenly clinic

Take a couple of aspirins and go to bed

because whoever you visit usually ends up dead

You enslave and change their names

Holding a cross while acting insane

I'll relax my mind and give you a pass

While you pray to your idols and enjoy your mass

Please don't forget one thing

The Messiah is powerful and black and to you He won't
sing

I guess I must have dozed off and dreamed

I had a nightmare it seems

People who preach we are all the same

Surely would not change someone else's name

FOOD

What's that smelling in the kitchen?

Is it some chicken?

Is that the third time this week?

Man, it's finger licking

Shake it bake it

Season it right

I can't wait to have

some chicken tonight

Is that collard greens too?

Now I know what to do

Hot cornbread

and iced tea brew

Macaroni and cheese

and apple pie

I'm ready to start eating

and that's no lie

But I'm only dreaming

and I don't know what to say

I got a cold hamburger and fries

I should have thrown away

Some warm orange soda

I forgot about

Now that my dream is over

I think I'll dine out

MR. PORK CHOP

Look out Mr. Pork Chop, I see you coming
Asking for sympathy like a fox
You can't look me in the eye
You are hard as a rock

How could you be a baby's daddy?
You are lazy with no job
You panhandle on my street
and the elderly you make plans to rob

When is the last time you read to your son
or took your baby mama out to eat?
I saw you last on 71st street
sitting on the curb eating some pig's feet

You got some fries and a pint of gin
but your son needs school clothes
He is hurt and ashamed of you
leaving his mama for some hoes

Mr. Pork Chop it is time to wake up

and reclaim your authority
The drugs won't help you
Your family should be your priority

Be an example to your son
There's not much time on the clock
Why lose a young brother
to the streets, holding a Glock?

The police shoot to kill
Save him and yourself
After all, you are his father
before you do anything else

Until you get this job done
Your woman is hurt and crying
Death is hiding behind your door
Please don't quit trying

Put the Pork Chop out of your life
Make that woman your loving wife
Sing a new song to gather
Become a new family that deals with strife

SELECTIVE AMNESIA

Do you remember what I told you
Not to go and what you should do
The response to my words
I know what I'm doing. Talk to the birds

The birds know when it's winter
Hear them sing, see them mentor
the ones leaving the nest
Obey what is best

And return in the spring
Happy to sing
Finding a place for their nest
Experience knows what's best

What about you?
How well did you do?
Did you take notes from them?
Or you had your eyes on him?

Keep your emotions under control

He will misuse you and rape your soul

I know this won't please yaw

But you have selective amnesia

OH, FATHER!

Oh Father, strengthen us to do righteousness

In my early days I must confess

I walk in a lie

I used the pagan name, why?

To celebrate pagan festivals

Eating food offered to idols

I was right in my own mind

The truth I could not find

Sunday, sun god worship everywhere

Preaching the commandments wasn't there

Father, how long will one follow

doctrines that are hollow?

Deny Your chosen ones their place

with pagan kingdoms based on race?

These kingdoms don't honor You

Mixing Romanish Greek philosophy, leavening what's true

The blind leading the blind

Poisoning the believer's mind

Afraid to study history

to help unlock the mystery

of who we are and where we come from

We need revelation to not stay dumb

What are you afraid of

if we double check?

We just want to avoid a wreck

It's your own soul that's at stake

Don't browbeat me, for heaven's sake

If I confirm what you say is true

I will willingly give you the respect due

But if I find out you are telling me a lie

You will answer to the Almighty, but I'll say goodbye

A Bible Study, should be the pure word with no mixture

Anything thing less is sorcerer's trickster

I must defend the word of the Most High

The verdict is out on what I saw

TREASURED SONGS

When the most treasured songs

warm my heart

With soothing and strengthening power

I soar above any problem

While keeping my feet on the ground

Changing my atmosphere

From the lyrics and melody

I am refreshed again

Oh, how I need patience

to trust my sense

and not just

my experience

Even though time

has slowed me down

I am happy

blessed and favored

I feel the twinkle

in my eyes

and a skip

in my steps

Moving with the sound

by clapping my hands

Praising and thanking

and exalting the Almighty

I have years of blessings

and heavenly peace

I must sing

and praise His Set-Apart Name

THE BLACK MESSIAH

Remove the stench of slavery from your mind

Scrape off the old plantation blueprint

Remove the poisonous, snake-bitten people from around you

I'm talking about you and no one else

How can you consider others with your neck in stocks?

Why do you use the same old ignorant language?

We shall overcome and black lives matter

Stained and shaped by an Uncle Tom's cabin mentality

Many are slayed by the oppressor's unsalable taste for blood

Especially your innocent sheepish blood

We have done everything these people demanded of us

They will never be satisfied with nothing less but our complete genocide

What does your life mean to you, Mr. and Mrs. Coon?

There is strength in numbers

But don't expect them to just stand by and watch

They will try to direct and produce the show

White supremacy today, tomorrow, and forever
is ingrained in every fiber of the oppressor's being
Spending billions of dollars to keep us dumb
Hoping, wishing, and praying to stay our oppressor

Many are called, but few are chosen
Wisdom is far from the simple minded
Your power lies deep within
and your special connection with the Almighty

Who is your messiah?
You have been looking outside of yourself
And you see your messiah everyday
When you let Him live in your soul

THE ADVERSARY

My fellowship is decreasing
while my enemies are increasing
Some blind ones will define you
and deny what is true

There is a growing measure
of knowledge absent of love
But will never let go
The real situation, they don't know

A foundationless effort
to spread Your work
Mixed with many mixtures
Race being a strong fixture

No matter what's the race
Oh, Most High, judge this case
No more blinded by man
Getting the strength to stand

On what my inner eyes see

Oh, Most High of justice, feed me

Some haters have hired

ones to put me in their fire

They surely will deny

the true reason why

they have shot many arrows

Strong souls who are narrow

Outwardly offering a welcoming smile

but will cast their net in a little while

I'm taking a respite not to fall

like King David did hiding from Saul

Learning to follow His commandments

for my spiritual growth and advancement

Growing stronger in this cause

Discovering His Sabbath and dietary laws

EVIL ONES

I don't want your god and I don't want your name

I just want my country which is my freedom of choice

I never signed myself over to you, neither did our fathers

You must give back what you stole or change the universal laws

You must honor my freedom of choice which is separated from you

You have never kept your word and you will never change

My word to the Indigenous Aboriginals you still dominate is:

If you want to buck dance, stay there

If you are a bed wench, stay there

If you are an Aunt Jemima, stay there

If you are an Uncle Remus, stay there

If you are a Boule, stay there

If you have sold your soul, stay there

If you are fearful, stay there

If you want to love the slave master religion, stay there

If you reject the truth, stay there, and leave us the hell alone

Keep your master happy, so he can pat you on the head

And step on your melanated soul, leaving you f***** up

Blinding your eyes from seeing the truth

Hidden deep in your soul and DNA

It whispers who you really are, and reveals the slave master's

lies and fraudulent evil deeds, wake up, wake up!

Separate yourselves from him, and the hopeless lost ones

Realize the Creator Almighty is your Boss

Tell your slave master:

I don't want your god

I don't want your Name

I just want my country

And you know where it is

And that's my freedom of choice

HELP SHARE TRUTH

Smiles of approval

from your smiling face

Expected support seems true

But from the heart, that's not the case

Baring the soul

to inform the seekers

Where are the ones

who is their brother's keeper?

Truth will find a way

to wake up the sleeping

It is written what we sow

we will be reaping

I don't know how

and I don't know where

I will share the truth

with those who really care

You may not understand

101

why I am so fervent

I have come to realize

that I am just a servant

SATURDAY MORNING

Speak to me, Almighty Most High

I incline my ear to Thee

Speak to me, Most High

My heart waits to see

There are so many opinions

There are so many different thoughts

There are so many interpretations

Father, you speak to my heart

Let the many have their opinions

Let all have their different thoughts

I shall follow the drum beat

That is within my heart

There are others who hear this drum beat

And with much prayer together, we

will all lay down our soul life

a blended labor this shall be

There's no super leader

There's no safety plan
Together we shall pay any price
Our life is in His hand

Not according to our concept
Nor according to our comfort zone
Neither to any irrational thinking
This flat earth shall embrace Your throne

THE OUTWARD ACT

The outward act can be forgiven

but the inward pain must be healed

Sun god day after sun god day

year after year; no change, no peace

The same promises I hear

once dynamic power

tried to sweep through the place

to help and lead us all

To His everlasting ways

now replaced by control

A mental habit to keep things new

What is stale and old and scripted for a few?

Quenching the spirits, of the old and the new

but out of a habit we all stay true

Like lambs being sheared

before the evening comes

We are placed in picking order

Like the blind leading the dumb

Just hang in there

and don't complain or whine

Even though you don't

Know If you could be blind

You are losing self-control

And that could be a sign

Separate the thinkers

so that others won't

Look a little deeper

Smile, but don't

The outward act

can be forgiven

But the inward pain

must be healed

I MUST TRAVEL ON

I must travel on a new journey

My heart and soul are one

Many people and many things

have fallen away and on the run

The Almighty, knows those who are His

His sheep will hear His voice

He is my Shepherd

and He is my only choice

I will not criticize

It's time to move on

My place of destination

tied to the work I have done

I hold no bitterness

to those who made me turn

My destination is heavenly

All what's left will burn

I see a new horizon

With more content and light
The storm is almost over
I'm in the last round of the fight

The Almighty of my salvation
The One I rely on and trust
is coming to recover us,
the righteous and the just

Thanking and thanking Him again
He gets all the esteem
I am so privileged
I am on His team

The time is running out
to make up your mind
Believe and trust in the Almighty
Another Savior, you won't find

A PRISONER OF IGNORANCE

A prisoner of ignorance
longing to be free
Like a bird with broken wings
grounded from reality

Stripped for the moment
by the games I see
Their pitcher threw a fast ball
A strike below my knees

I must act correctly
with a hidden life, new and supreme
and turn away for any drama
I know I've been redeemed

Love my enemies
and not feel sorry for them
Or trying to explain
every little whim
The prisoner of ignorance
finally, is free

I look to no one

but the Almighty and me

BE MY LIFE

Be my life forever
Shine your light within
Night and day forever
You are my only friend

Be my life forever
Be the life within
Keep the light within me
That never grows dim

Be my life forever
You are my only friend
Let your set-apart spirit
Shine deep within

I'm asking the Almighty to help me
He is like the eternal wind
Teach me Your royal laws
Keep me from sin

I'm tired of religion

It's just a dead end

It never fed my hunger

The world and it's teaching blend

Silver and gold, I have not

The food in the cupboard is thin

I'm working temporarily

and fleeing from sin

I won't mark up my body

It's the temple of my friend

The Almighty is my master

None other can come in

This is my testimony

The ceremonial and dietary laws

Hidden by religion

Read the hidden clause

The law and testimony

The feast of unleavened bread

I am one of His sons

The Almighty is my everlasting Head

SUBDUE THE FLESH

Strengthening our spirit

will weaken our flesh

Make the flesh submit to the spirit

and have peace and rest

Fervent prayer strengthens the spirit

Breaking the commandments helps the flesh

Empower the spirit

The righteous path to success

The key to dealing with this life

is a strong, righteous spirit

Created and empowered by the Almighty

Will you believe it?

Even though we experience falling and repenting

Repenting and falling

in a cycle of despair

The flesh keeps calling

We learn to pray and seek to overcome

Fighting to be free

We must kill this flesh

Is more than talk, you see

The core of our struggles

is which one will win

The flesh or the commandments

will decide your end

BE HUMBLE

So, you see something

Don't think you have seen it all

You should be more teachable

and understand you can fall

Talents and gifts are distributed

to as many as the Almighty would choose

So, don't boast in what you have

cause that portion you could lose

Listen to your words

and all your explanations

A lampstand burns oil

that is a basic revelation

A candle does not burn oil

but you continued to say

the English translation of the bible

on that word candlestick has lost its way

The oil represents the Spirit

not a bunch of waxed sticks
Do a little more studying
oil and candles don't mix

Man should not live by bread alone
but by the Almighty's living Word
Only He knows the mysteries
and much you haven't heard

Try to be more humble
Treasure what portion you have
Reason with your brothers
Deep wounds need healing salve

Why accuse each other
while the people are lost and dying?
The Almighty's sheep are being destroyed
See His meek ones praying and crying

Whatever we have is for His sheep
And not worry about our feelings
But faithfully labor and feed his people
and care for their spiritual healing

THE HYBRIDS

A hybrid and malignant race
Cruel, evil, and corrupted
Made by the experiment from the fallen ones
The good and righteous disrupted

Lofty, full of pride, and unremorseful
working and teaching mysteries in women's lives
to separate them from their Almighty
Making the daughters of men their wives

Producing hybrid children
Neither man nor divine
Now giants in the land thirsty
Killing whoever they find

The Heavens warned man
from these ones, turn away
But they would not listen
to what the Prophets had to say

Rebuked by the Highest of all

and a time limit has been set

His Spirit will not always strive with man

so, the rain of judgement did they get

It rained many days and many nights

Now their bodies lie beneath the deep

Judgement has rained on them

What they have sowed they have reaped

By spenser @ unplash

JUSTICE AND IN-JUSTICE

MURDERED MAN'S LAST PRAYER

Kill and smear

The end is near

Consider your ways

That soul doth pray

To a righteous Judge

Before his last breath

His soul prayed to rest

In the arms of the Almighty

Send my murderers to hell's fire

By a righteous Judge

DECEPTION

Words fall off your lips like butter

Melting in the heat of deception

A secret life hidden from mirrors

Regretting, lamenting your life's direction

A hungry soul smiling in pain

Stuck in a loveless life

Killing the fire within

Betrayal cuts like a knife

Tie the rockets to the knees

Take the rope off the neck

Kiss the water from the eyes

And burn the joker in the deck

Call the soldier back to arms

Who's fighting for his life

Stop the games on the computer

Learn what it means to be a wife

MR. POLICE #1

Take the bullseye

Off my back

And the rope

Off my neck

Extra guns on the rack

Load 'em up for the blacks

Hunt 'em down like a dog

Break down their doors

And their walls

Plant the drugs in their cars

Then meet the boys at the bar

Buy a round for the day

We put another nigga away

Lada dee lada da

Lada dee lada da

Lada dee lada da

That's our song in the bar

Another round at the bar

Give the shooter a cigar

Lada dee lada da

That's our song in the bar

MELEK'S BLUES #1

Dancing on razor blades

Engulfing phagocytes eating wounds

Predatory starlight

Exposes my life

Hide me Ohio river

Bathe me mighty Mississippi

Change my DNA

Portrait of light

Dancing on volcanoes

Inhaling burning sulfur

Predatory moonlight

Exposes my night

Hide me eagle's nest

Bathe me cirrostratus clouds

Lose my pellagra

Portrait photic

Never again to identify

In name, thought or living

To the slave master's children

Repent less, theft, and hate

MR. POLICE #2

Take the bullseye off my back

And the rope off my neck

Extra guns on the rack

Load 'em up for the blacks

Hunt 'em down like a dog

Break down their doors and their walls

Buy a round for the day

We put another nigga away

Another round at the bar

Give the shooter a cigar

Hunt 'em down like a dog

Make 'em squeal like a hog

Ground and pound 'em in the head

He ha another nigga is dead

Another blessed day

We're putting more niggas away!

Lada dee lada da

Lada dee lada da

Lada dee lada da

That's our song in the bar!

PROSECUTOR

Your lips move

but I hear no sound

When your lips are closed

I hear parts

of the same story

Keeping me in subjection

and stealing my glory

You make your truth a tool

to make yourself a stallion

and me a mule

Working the consciousness

of bias media blitz

To cleanse the hands

that shed innocent blood

Spelled on the marquee

A new sacrifice

For the secret club

But drums of my fathers

and the shofar of my elders

will never die

NO JUSTICE

We have appealed to the rulers

and to the judges of this land

They have closed their ears to justice

Wherever we are in this land

Every generation who looked up to Heaven

Every generation who heard the righteous angel's song

Every generation where justice is hidden

Suffered us to sing this song

Help us, Almighty

Help us, we pray

Send your favor and justice

Don't let our lives cry today

Don't let our lives cry today

Don't let our lives cry today

Send your favor and justice

Don't let our lives cry today

Many years the rulers made promises

Many years the rulers made laws

Many years the Judges made rulings

And nothing has truly changed thus far

Help us, Almighty

Help us, we pray

Send your favor and justice

Don't let our lives cry today

Don't let our lives cry today

Don't let our lives cry today

Send your favor and justice

Don't let our lives cry today

MELEK'S BLUES #2

We arrived at masa's plantation

near the black river road

Lawd, I hope he will be a good Massa

I heard them call this place Sumter, South Carolina

It's mighty hot out there

I got clothes, shoes, and a burlap sack

You really want to know how I felt

when I saw what they call cotton

My, my, I see cotton everywhere

I wonder who is going to pick it

I believe this was one of Melek's songs

Sometimes after we worked all day

Sun up 'til sundown, Massa

made us dance for him

'cause some of his friends

wanted some entertainment, and say

"Dance, nigga, dance or get whipped"

So, I danced with the strength I had left

from working in the field all day

We danced a secret dance to curse our enemies

They are cursed forever

But our indigenous aboriginal sins are temporary

Never again to identify name, thought, or living

to the slave Massa's and their children

Repent less, theft, and hate

I pray that my grandsons and grand daughters

Would finally wake up and realize, that they are

The apple of the Almighty's eye

PRISONS

Prisons without walls
where maritime laws
secretly invade common law
producing the color of law

Making people persons
a creature of corporate law
Duped into countless adhesion contracts
Giving life to fictitious straw men

A matrix of deception
enriching those who already have
Whose diabolical and immoral system
rape and plunder of the unlearned masses

Heartless, calculating, and wicked devils
Fearless in greed, deception, and robbery
Making slaves out of free men
who live and need your matrix to survive

In this prison without walls

where maritime laws

secretly invade common law

producing the color of law

CANCER OF THE EARTH

Be prepared daily to die
Each moment your will is being killed
by chem trails falling from the sky
Then you wash and cook your food with fluoride

They remind you to get your vaccines
Are they mixed with death and monkey spleens?
Man, I can no longer go with the flow
While most of the food is labeled GMO

Why are my taxes so high -
Payroll, state, county, city, and everything I buy?
More and more promises from politicians
They should live in the darkest prisons

The bankers never gave a loan
They should be jailed and overthrown
Charging interest on your cash value
Making money out of air, you scoundrel damn you

The fall of the white man

Is right before our eyes

It's raining in their houses

Can you hear their animal cries?

The meat is red and juicy

but the blood is caked and dried

All that's left of you beasts

are the remains of your hides

Your tricks are no longer hidden, and the source of your
smiles are lies

We are realizing who we truly are

and we are beseeching and demanding for

the Almighty's army to fill the skies

CURSES

A cup full of curses

our fathers were given to drink

Written in the book of Deuteronomy

Our fathers' sins and ours are linked

The cup is still not empty

We have been disciplined for many years

Take a close look at our people

It brings a grown man to tears

Our young men are going to prison

like it's the place to be

The fathers try to talk to them

but some are also there, you see

It's not our whole nation

who have taken this path

But the brothers who remain

forgot who they are you do the math

Few brothers in our households

A broken family trees
Some sisters don't want a brother
because some women wear men's pants you see

This cup full of curses
Is still before us today
We must honor the contract with the Most High
Repent and watch what we say

Before this will happen
we must fully drink this cup
It will separate the sheep from the goats
The meek from the corrupt

Now I understand why we are treated so badly
and why we are the tail and not the head
It is because we broke the contract
with the Almighty who raises the dead

The Willie Lynch letter
will give you a clue
Psalm chapter eighty-three
is all about you

EXAMINE?

Why would we not examine

the impotent traditional view?

No longer to take for granted

what so-called leaders say is true

Leaders telling us to integrate

Why not just respect everyone?

The scripture says, "Come out from among them,

And let the Father's will be done

All the wealth in this world

won't buy eternal life

More laws to regulate us

won't eradicate all strife

We all must pay for how we lived

whether we are a sheep or a goat

It can feel like a fiery razor blade

aiming at your throat

Soon you might say your last goodbyes

as your weapons melt to the ground

If we search all over the earth

will we find you still around?

Maybe heaven has had enough

and hopefully you realize

Is that why you aim your weapons

toward the Righteous One in the sky?

Is righteousness in your store

or is there deception and lies amok?

Do you sow discord

and then pass the buck?

Why would we not examine

the impotent traditional view?

And not take for granted

what so-called leaders say is true?

GENUINE

I can say this
and I can say that
I have only one talent
and that is a fact

Why should I portray
something I don't have?
Will I appear to wise men
without some healing salve?

How about giving myself a title
and think highly of myself?
But in the wisdom of the Heavens
I have only a little wealth

So, I will just be satisfied
with what the Almighty has measured
And not compare me to others
but what I am given I will treasure

Every day I must seek

the wisdom from above

the Almighty's, laws, and commands

And take strength from His love

THIEVES

Thieves hiding the truth

like dogs of war

An army of wicked workers

you know who you are

Coveting and bearing false witness

Directing the media to lie

Relentless effort to confuse

The truth you defy

Rewrote history

to cover up your sins

And what you have done in the dark

is no longer hidden in your den

Unconscionable, soulless beasts

Representatives of hell

Seeds of the serpent

You will reap what you sell

For over two-thousand years

you've had time to make things right
Instead you corrupted yourselves
and turn people's day into night

You are unworthy of more time
and your day of reckoning has come
You and your seed are under the feet
of His will that shall be done

A BUCKET OF COMMON SENSE

A bucket of common sense

Oh, indigenous people

Pour your ignorance down the drain

and your allegiance to Folly-land will die

Did you not get the memo?

And recognize your enemies' plans

The evidence is everywhere

To keep you tied up in knots

Every group of people

Have their own nation

Every nation has their own land

Handed down through their fathers

Stop worrying about everyone else

Why be maids and butlers for this world?

Take that time to build up your Tribe

And your twelve Tribes will become a nation

A nation of indigenous aboriginals

Whose king is The Almighty

Magnify His Name

He is the Creator King Eternal

He will force all our enemies

Down the road of tears

They will be humbled at His coming

We will no longer have to fear

Hold tight your bucket of common sense

Oh, indigenous people

Keep pouring your ignorance down the drain

And your allegiance to Babylon will die

REST

Rest in Your embrace

Rest in Your warm embrace

We are prodigal sons

Please let us come back home

to rest in our Father's embrace

We no longer desire to eat

the food fed to the swine

Father, we realize that we're

just pilgrims in this world

We have worshipped

the idols of the nations

We have worshipped

at their festivals and feasts

Holidays and entertainments

Our mind and our history have been lost

Our hearts are waxed cold

We worship all the idols in the land

Your commandments we despise

We as Your people worship lies

and your warnings we ignore

We trust Babylon the whore

Father, you have a few

Who still listen to You

A remnant growing throughout all the lands

Who no longer worship Babylon

Her witchcraft and mind control

We are the genuine indigenous aboriginals of old

A set-apart nation and priests to the Most High

Now we like to live in Your warm embrace

THE CITY

The city of darkness is fading away
and the residue of its power is falling
The inhabitants of Folly-land's love for their idols
will not save them from being burned to the ground

The songs and the dancing have ceased in her
and their mighty ones who have earthly fame
Their pagan worship and idolatrous holidays
will not help Babylon cover her shame

Falling, Falling, Babylon Falling, Falling down
Falling, Falling, Babylon Falling, Falling down
Hiding deep in the caves and rocks
But, still hear the heavenly chariots sound

With the end of Babylon, a new age has come
Chosen ones are saying, His will be done
The Almighty's rule is now on earth
The struggle is over, and the victory is won

AGAIN

Another soul put to rest

Riding a bike in a free land

Stopped and was interrogated

in the land of Babylon

Left his home whole

But now he is severed

Six wolves ate him

causing his painful screams

Someone was smart

and took a video

of his body badly broken

from riding his bike in Babylon

Callous, hard, cold, and mean

is what we face every day

Those sworn to protect

disconnect us from our necks

Evil laughs and think it is over

But that's not the case

Thou shalt not murder!

The Heavenly Court you must face

RECERTIFICATION

In an old recertification class

I wish I could have taken a pass

I feel uneasy in this realm

Where I sit, the graphics are dim

The letter states I must come

to lose my licenses would be dumb

I have four in all

so why am I sitting in the back near the wall?

Ten hours I need a year

to lend my body and my ears

I hope I can stay awake

Now my legs are beginning to ache

Sitting in a plastic chair for ten hours

Wow I need the power

to get through this day

and enjoy this sunshine in May

At least I can dream

I need some coffee and cream

The pastries look tasty

This one is sweet and pasty

Now I just need to settle down

and not be distracted by the sound

of private conversations

putting down a coworker's reputation

In this recertification class

I have a lot to lose if I don't pass

At least I think I will

I hope this will help me pay my bills

FORGET ABOUT

Forget about how you look
Just clothe yourself with truth
Keep your mind washed
Bare righteous fruit

Forget about what others think
They have no power to heal
They are propping up
What they think is real

Forget about how you feel
We have our ups and downs
Tomorrow is a new day
The almighty's messengers are encamped all around

Forget about the pain
You carry in your heart
Each day it gets a little better
Soon the pain will depart

Forget about Christianity

It was forced upon you

This European culture

History shows it's untrue

Forget about being simple

Show yourself approved

Because much of the truth

has been hidden or removed

Forget about being lonely

It's the cost of knowing the truth

Keep on watching and praying

Know that the chickens will come home to roost

TRANSPARENCY

We have many Nobel Prize winners

and many new discoveries and medical inventions

Just about everything from A to Z

But one more thing I must mention

This is our desperate need

Which is easy to create but always delayed

A child could advise a scholar

without being paid

The people of this world

have many books and much knowledge

and there are some smart people

who never went to college

But with all the news and many opinions

talk shows and religious events

I like to ask an honest question

Tell me where love went

We are told there is nothing to hide

Be patient and let us be

What happened to this one word?

TRANSPARENCY!

A NEW DAY

A new day is dawning in our lives
The lost connection to our history and ancient fathers
has mysteriously been infused solidly within
Wow, it was lost but it is found today

No longer shall we be ruled
by black faces with white minds
Whose loyalty is to Massa boss?
and all the slaves with benefits who agree

Those who represent a dark past
The future does not know your name
and the wise among us feel pity for you
because we understand the Almighty's commands

Concerning His prophecy being fulfilled
Right before our eyes
The only empire that will remain
is our Maker the Creator Almighty

A new day is dawning in our hearts

Murder and oppression will stop

A mysterious phenomenon of infusing each day

The understanding of our secret past

NEW INFORMATION

New information scares some
and can threaten our comfort zone
When it does, we cannot avoid admitting
we were lied to and oh, how that hurts

Truth can be uncomfortable and frightening
But after a while it can become soothing to our soul
A mind being unshackled and freed from indoctrination
can cause our puppet masters to become unemployed

Is this the first step in being liberated
from doctrines created to keep us dumb?
Don't ask many questions, just believe
and be obedient to whatever we teach

I received some information the other day
New information that opened my eyes
It left me shocked and petrified
I have lived 40-plus years believing this lie

The whole New Testament is a lie

When you research the authors of the New Testament

Abelard Reuchlin history book

is a very good place to start

AUTHOR'S BIO

My name is Leroy Peoples Jr©R and I wrote my first poem 58 years ago, motivated by the rejection of my first love. Throughout the years, I have envisioned writing a book, and reading select portions in the public domain.

After graduating from high school, I attended and graduated from trade school in the technical field. I attended over 1 year of college and have a ton of life experiences.

I am 70 years old and have two lovely daughters, Leia and Kesha. I have a strong stepson who I expect to surpass me in every way. I respect his privacy, so I will call him "V" for victory. My lovely wife, Doris J. is the love of my life, my partner, friend, and more.

I am of few words, but my hope is for those who read my poetry book will receive inspiration to move forward, with new information, enlightenment, spiritual guidance, and to usher you closer to the Creator, Almighty, Most High.

I would like to thank all of my family members and in-laws for their encouragement, prayers, and positive thoughts. I would also like to thank all my haters for your consistent disbelief in me. You have made me stronger and wiser.

Peace and success to all my positive readers.

Roy P.J.